Suzuki® Violin School

VIOLIN PART
VOLUME 10

Copyright © 1976 Dr. Shinichi Suzuki
Sole publisher for the entire world except Japan:
Summy-Birchard Inc.
exclusively distributed by
Warner Bros. Publications
15800 N.W. 48th Avenue, Miami, FL 33014
All rights reserved   Printed in U.S.A.

ISBN 0-87487-226-X

The Suzuki name, logo and wheel device
are trademarks of Dr. Shinichi Suzuki used
under exclusive license by Summy-Birchard, Inc.

INTRODUCTION

FOR THE STUDENT: This material is part of the worldwide Suzuki Method of teaching. Companion recordings should be used with these publications. In addition, there are piano accompaniment books that go along with this material.

FOR THE TEACHER: In order to be an effective Suzuki teacher, a great deal of ongoing education is required. Your national Suzuki association provides this for its membership. Teachers are encouraged to become members of their national Suzuki associations and maintain a teacher training schedule, in order to remain current, via institutes, short and long term programs. You are also encouraged to join the International Suzuki Association.

FOR THE PARENT: Credentials are essential for any teacher that you choose. We recommend you ask your teacher for his or her credentials, especially listing those relating to training in the Suzuki Method. The Suzuki Method experience should be a positive one, where there exists a wonderful, fostering relationship between child, parent and teacher. So choosing the right teacher is of the utmost importance.

In order to obtain more information about the Suzuki Method, please contact your country's Suzuki Association, the International Suzuki Association at 3-10-15 Fukashi, Matsumoto City 390, Japan, The Suzuki Association of the Americas, 1900 Folsom, #101, Boulder, Colorado 80302 or Summy-Birchard Inc., c/o Warner Bros. Publications Inc., 15800 N.W. 48th Avenue, Miami, Florida 33014, for current Associations' addresses.

CONTENTS

Concerto in D Major

コンチェルト
ニ長調

Wolfgang Amadeus Mozart
Joachim - Suzuki

Rondeau
Andante grazioso (♩=ca.63)

Andante grazioso

Allegro ma non troppo

The First Movement
Allegro

第一楽章
アレグロ

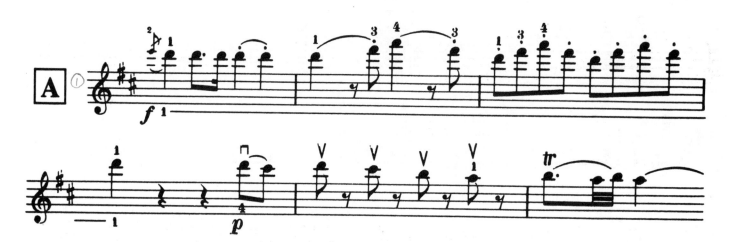

Point of Practice　　学習の仕方

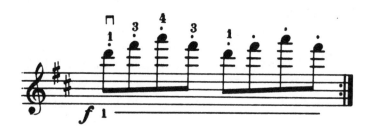

Shape the left hand properly (see B of the Third Movement), and use the bow a little distance from the frog, always keeping the right elbow moving correctly.

It is important to obtain beautiful sound not only in the contrasting *f* and *p* parts but also in bringing out the theme.

I would like to suggest to those who cannot play a trill correctly, that if the first finger is held down unconsciously, the second and third fingers will not move quickly enough. It is out of the question to try to play a trill with the first finger fixed firmly on the string. For the purpose of practice, raise the first finger and then place the second and third fingers on the string before starting to play the trill. This practice is also very effective for a trill starting with the second finger.

左手の正しい形に注意。弓の元の少し上の方で弾き、正確なひじの動きを忘れてはならない。(第3楽章Bを参照)

f のところと *p* のところの美しいコントラスを表現する練習、工夫が大切で、また主題を力強く美しい音にする練習が必要。

トリルのうまくできない人のために私の経験を記して置こう。気がつかぬままに1の指を押えたままでトリルするのは、2、3の指の動きをにぶらせる。ましてや1の指を強く押えたままでトリルを弾こうとしてもできない。ここは弾く前に1の指を離して2、3の指を押え、トリルをするように練習をしてみてください。2の指から音を出す場合でもこの練習は鮮かなトリルをつくるよい方法です。

指の準備

Point of Practice　学習の仕方

In the beginning, practice at about half speed.

最初は倍くらいテンポをおそく練習をはじめること。

指の準備（準備とともに１の指をはなす）
Prepare the fingers and immediately raise
the first finger.

Somewhat advanced pupils, beginning to play up to speed are likely to fluctuate in tempo and in pitch. This means that there has been insufficient practice and still more careful study is necessary.

少し熟練して本来のテンポで弾きはじめるとき，多くの人の欠点として，拍子がせき込みがちになってくることと，音程が不正確になりやすいことです。この２つのことをマスターできないかぎりまだ練習不足ですから，よく注意して学習すること。

Point of Practice　学習の仕方

Start bowing with the upper part of the bow.
The fingering given above the score is Joachim's indication, and the fingering below is that based on my own practice. Whichever fingering is adopted must be practiced carefully.

Shifting Exercises for Second and Third Positions.

弓の上部で弾きはじめる。
音符の上に記した指づかいはヨアヒムのボしたもので，五線の下の指づかいは私が試みている指づかいです。熟練すればいずれでもよいかと思う。

３および２ポジションの移り方の訓練。

Point of Practice

Even if pupils have learned the notes, they should remember that, without good tone and rhythm they cannot claim to be able to play. With this in mind, they should listen carefully to all aspects of virtuosos' performances.

The sixteenth notes should be played evenly and with beautiful tone. Most pupils are inclined to play too fast.

学習の仕方

音符が一応弾けるようになっても，音の表現が鮮かで，テンポがしっかりしていないうちはまだ弾けないのだということを忘れてはならない。このことをいつも自分に言いきかせ，名人達の演奏を部分的によく観察して聞く必要がある。

このところはテンポを正しく，16分音符が美しく楽しく鳴ることが必要です。多くの人ははやくなりがちに弾いています。

Raise the first finger.

この場合はビブラートするために1の指を離して弾くこと。左手の形を正しくたもち，指はなるべく ⇘ よりも ⇊ の方向で押える。

For the purpose of vibrato, play this note with the first finger raised. Shape the left hand correctly. The left hand fingers should be placed on the string like this: ⇘ rather than like this: ⇊

美しいビブラートとトリルの訓練を正しいテンポで試みる。
Try to play vibrato and trill beautifully at the correct tempo.

テンポを正しく弾く練習。
Keep the tempo steady.

音符の下の指づかいは私の試みている指づかいです。
The fingering shown below the notes is based on my own practice.

Point of Practice　　学習の仕方

この2箇所のテンポが速すぎて乱れる人が多い。落ちついて弾けるように
熟練すること。G線の1の指を離さないように。

Many pupils play these pairs of notes too fast to keep the tempo steady.
Learn to play them without haste.
Do not raise the first finger off the G-string.

Point of Practice　　学習の仕方

Practice for smooth change of strings with beautiful
tone and good intonation by using the upper third of
the bow.

弓の上部を使い、弓巾せまくはっきりとした音で、鮮か
な移弦の練習と美しい表現の練習をすること。

G *brillante*

Point of Practice　学習の仕方

はじめにトリルなしで練習し熟練すること。
Practice without the trill at first.

Continue to practice until both the ascending and descending notes are performed accurately. Keep the descending notes steady.

上行と下行が正しく弾けるまで訓練する必要がある。一般に下行が不安定になりやすい。

４，３の指の正確な音程がとれるようにすること。

Learn to get the exact interval between the fourth and third fingers.

事前に２，３の指の準備の練習をする。
Before practicing, silently prepare the second and third fingers.

Practice the following in the indicated order.

(A)　練習順序　(B)

Fine performance can never be expected unless constant training is continued every day for at least a month. Do not forget that virtuosos' brilliant performances are the result of many years' persevering efforts.

Pattern of Practice.

少なくとも１か月くらい毎日忘れずに訓練しなければ鮮かな演奏はできないでしょう。名人達の鮮かな演奏は長い間の努力によって生れていることを忘れてはならない。

Place the second and third fingers together on the string without using the bow, and test the pitch of each note. If all pitches are found to be accurate in five successive trials, correct intonation can be expected. Then try to play the actual trill.

試みに弓を使わないで２，３の指を瞬間に押えそれぞれの音の音程を調べてごらんなさい。５回とも正確だったらトリルが正確にできるでしょう。それからトリルをやってみてください。

After the above practice, proceed to the following exercise.

以上のような練習を経て次のように練習を試みるのがよいでしょう

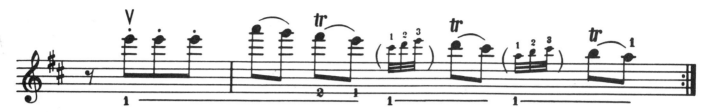

Continue to practice until you achieve exact pitches instantaneously with the first, second and third fingers. In moving the fingers, concentrate on the second finger and fix the first finger according to the position of the second finger.

1，2，3の指を瞬間に押えて正しい音程であるように訓練する。感覚は2の指を中心位置として移し，1の指は2の指にしたがって位置をつくる。

Point of Practice　　学習の仕方

Make the aim of practice here to fix the second position steadily, to change strings accurately and to produce refined sound in the *p* passages.

第2ポジションの確実性をやしなうことと移弦の訓練，および *p* のときの音形の美しさを訓練することの2つを目標に努力すべきである。

四度を正確にひくこと。
Try to play the fourths accurately.

Point of Practice　　学習の仕方

弓の練習
Exercise for Bowing.

Practice the notes exactly as they are printed, to attain perfect accuracy in playing each note so that the whole passage is executed correctly however often it may be repeated.

音符のとおりひき，1音づつ立派に熟練した上，正しく何回でもひけるように試みること。

Practice without the trill at first.

最初トリルなしで正しく弾けるように。

この3の指の準備がおそくなりがちであるから，Dを弾いた瞬間に3の指を準備する練習を行なう。この訓練ができればトリルができる第一歩に入る。

Train the third finger to be prepared the moment D is played. This practice is the first step in playing trills.

Exercise for Accurate Tempo.

正しいテンポを守る練習。

Pupils are apt to hurry and accordingly find difficulty in playing. It would be easier by far to play strictly at the correct tempo.

一般にテンポがはやくなりやすく，そのためにいっそうむずかしくなる。正しいテンポを守ればはるかに弾きやすくなります。

Point of Practice　　　学習の仕方

3 の指に 2 の指をつける
Keep the second finger close
to the third finger.

Point of Practice　　　学習の仕方

Fundamental Exercise
基本練習

このトリルへの移り方がなかなかむずかしい。Gの2の指のあと瞬間的に2，3のトリルの指の準備をする練習をしなければいけません。そのためには次の練習をすすめます。

It is rather difficult to go into this trill. Sufficient practice is necessary to prepare the second and third fingers for the trill, immediately after playing G with the second finger. The following exercise is recommended for this purpose:

はじめゆっくり Play slowly in the beginning.

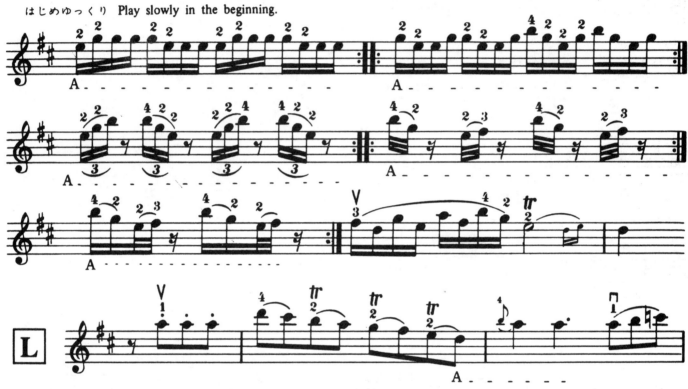

Point of Practice　　学習の仕方

この練習が正しく弾けなければいけません。どのポジションでも美しくそろうようになってからトリルの練習にすすんでください。

練習をしていく上の参考。

ポジションを移ったときのトリルがきれいにできないのは，多くの場合，まずポジションを移る手の速さが定まらないということ，それから左手の形が移る以前の形と変わってしまうという2つの欠点が原因です。このような比較的やさしい譜で，鮮かさ，美しさを学んでほしいと思います。

It is important to be able to play this exercise correctly. Do not proceed to the trill exercise before beautiful sound is achieved in every position.
Practical advice for this exercise:
Imperfect trills after a position change are often due to two causes: the hand doesn't shift positions quickly enough; and the left hand is not shaped properly when the position change is made. Relatively easy exercises such as the above example would be helpful in attaining brilliant and beautiful expression.

Cadenza
カデンツ

Point of Practice　　学習の仕方

Fundamental Exercise
基本練習

Pay special attention to the shape of the left hand and fingers at the position shift. (See B of the Third Movement.)

ポジションを移るときに左手の形，指の形に注意。(第3楽章B を参照のこと)

Exercise for the Fourth Finger and Shape of the Left Hand. (The first finger should be raised.)

4 の指と左手の形の訓練。(1 の指を離す)

この 2 の指で押えた音D が開放弦にひびいて鳴るようにし，その余韻が次の音を弾くまでほしい。

The second finger should place D where the open string resonates so that the sound continues until the next note is played.

To make the intervals accurate, practice slowly at first, omitting the slurs.

音程を正しくするためにはじめはスラーをとってゆっくり練習すること。

Try to produce beautiful legato sound with accurate intervals.

レガートで美しく，音程がそろうように。

余韻が美しく鳴るように訓練。
Make the tones vibrate beautifully.

速くひきがちなので，滑らかに本来のテンポで弾くことができるよう注意。
Be careful about the tempo, which is likely to get too fast, and try to play smoothly in tempo.

calando

静かに
Softly.

Pを十分練習する。
Do enough practice in *p*.

2の指に1の指をつける
Keep the first finger close to the second finger.

Dの音程を正しく
Fix the pitch of the note D accurately.

美しく歌うように。
Play beautifully as if singing.

in tempo

レガートに弾けるように。
Learn to play legato.

2の指に3の指をつける
Keep the third finger close to the second finger.

in tempo

重音は美しい音のバランスを練習。
Try to balance the beautiful tones of the double stop.

It is necessary to acquire, through training, the technique and security for shifting quickly from the first position to the fifth position. Shape the left hand correctly in the fifth position. (See B of the Third Movement.)

第1ポジションから第5ポジションへの敏速な移動と安定性を訓練し獲得することが必要です。このとき第5ポジションの左手の形を正しくするように。(第3楽章B参照)

In changing positions, make sure to place the first finger close to where the second finger was placed.
This applies to both ascending and descending figures.

このポジション移動のとき1の指が2の指についているかどうかを見るように。これは上行，下行とも同じことです。

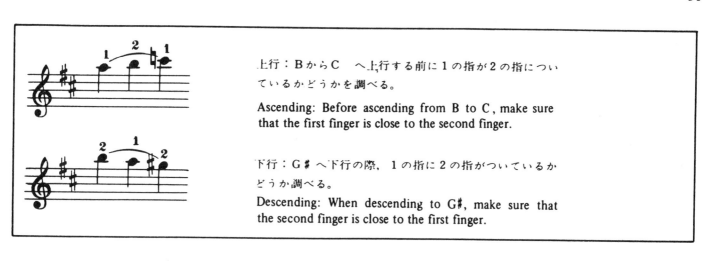

上行：BからC　へ上行する前に1の指が2の指についているかどうかを調べる。

Ascending: Before ascending from B to C, make sure that the first finger is close to the second finger.

下行：G♯へ下行の際，1の指に2の指がついているかどうか調べる。

Descending: When descending to G♯, make sure that the second finger is close to the first finger.

p scherzando

四度を正しく練習すること。
Practice the fourth accurately.

Fix the intonation of the fourth accurately.
四度の音程を正しく。

cresc.

基本

この音を
正しく
Play this note accurately.

cresc.

f

1の指に2の指をつける
Keep the second finger close to the first finger.

1 の指を正しく
Place the first finger correctly.

指の正しい位置の練習と 1 の指をつけたままの訓練。
Exercise for Correct Placement of Fingers without Raising the First Finger.

1 の指に 2 の指をつける
Keep the second finger close to the first finger.

Practice the following with the left hand shaped correctly.　左手の形を正しくし，そのままで弾く練習。

五度
Fifth

34

Keep the first finger
close to the second finger.

Keep the second finger
close to the third finger.

Fundamental Exercise

Fundamental Exercise

Fundamental Exercise

The Second Movement
Andante Cantabile
第二楽章
アンダンテ　カンタービレ

Point of Practice　　　学習の仕方

左手の指の形が丸くそして弦に対して直角に近いくらいに押える。

Curve the third finger and place it almost at a right angle to the string.

Study and improve the shape of the left hand. (See B of the Third Movement.)

左手の形の研究と矯正を行なう。(第3楽章B参照)

Point of Practice　　　学習の仕方

sfp は、sf スフォルツァンド（特に強く）の後すぐ p で弾くという意味です。sf の音の強さはその曲の感覚をよく考えて適切に弾くべきです。

sfp means that *p* must be played immediately after *sf* (sforzando; especially with force). The degree of *sf* should be determined according to the character of the passage.

Point of Practice

Play this passage as expressively as you can. Compare your performance with those of virtuosos and study their tempo as well as their beautiful sound and vibrato. One of the surest ways to improve is to study excellent performances, comparing them with your own performance in four aspects: tempo, tone, pitch and vibrato. By constantly studying virtuosos' recordings, comparing them with your own performance in these four points, you will come to realize after what careful study they attained their accuracy and beauty. I expect pupils to understand step by step their execution, such as handling of the bow, speed of bowing and action of the right elbow.

学習の仕方

この美しいメロディーをどれだけ美しい音とテンポで弾けるかを試してください。テンポ、音の美しさ、ビブラートの美しさの研究など、名人達の演奏を聞いて自分と比較してみてください。

常に優れたものと自分とを、テンポ、音色、音程、ビブラートの4つの点に分けて比較して研究するのが上達の1つの道です。すぐれたレコードをこのように部分的に比較して聞いているうちに、名人達がどのように細心な研究をして、正しく美しく弾いているかを知るようになるでしょう。また、彼らの弓の扱かい方、スピードの具合、右ひじの運びなどまで、その奏法をだんだんに感じるようになってください。

この2オクターブの音を正しくひく。
Play this two-octave interval accurately.

Point of Practice　　学習の仕方

(弦) D－A－D－E （2の指に3の指をつける）
Strings: D-A-D-E (Keep the third finger close to the second finger.)

音程を正確にするために練習
Exercise for Correct Intervals.

Point of Practice　　学習の仕方

Note: 1) Pupils are apt to press the bow too firmly on the string when they play the notes in higher positions on the G string. Enough care must be taken so that the bow is used on the string in the same way as if tuning on the open string. Many pupils usually produce excellent sound in tuning, and they should apply the same control of the bow and sound to all the notes they play.

Note: 2) Left hand fingers should be rounded on the fingerboard, almost at a right angle to the string. The relation of the string and the finger should be ⟋ rather than ⟍, and in higher positions the angle must be ⊥.

注意：(1)G弦の高いポジションの音を弾くとき，一般的に弾く弓で弦を押えすぎるようです。十分注意して開放弦で調弦するときの弓と同じように弦を鳴らすべきです。調子を合わせるとき多くの人が実に上手に弦を鳴らしており，そのときの弓の加減，弦の鳴り方をそのままにすべての音の鳴り方に用いることが必要です。

(2)左手の指の形が指板の上で，まるく，指の方向がなるべく弦に向って直角に近ずくくらいに心がけるべきです。⟋よりも⟋の方がよく，高いポジションのときにはさらに⊥となる。

Be careful about the shape of the left hand while practicing. (See B of the Third Movement.)

左手の形に注意し練習すること。（第3楽章Bを参照）

38

Cadenza
カデンツ

Point of Practice　　学習の仕方

2，4の指に1，3の指をつける。
(Keep the first and the third fingers close to the second and fourth fingers.)

音程を正確にする
The intervals must be made accurate.

を押えたとき同時に左手指の形を熟練する。
When the fingers are placed for these notes, also try to improve the shape of the left hand.

を押える訓練をする。
Learn to place the finger properly for this note.

できるだけ練習をおこたらないように。
Continue to practice till you can play well.

半音　　半音

くり返し練習する
Practice repeatedly.

半音　半音　　　半音　半音

注意：重音はゆっくり正確な音程で練習する。弓巾は少なくてよく、弓で弦を押えつけぬこと。

Note: Practice double stops slowly with accurate intervals. Play with short bowing and do not press the string with the bow.

(Fixing of the first finger for G# is made easier by keeping the third finger on the string.)

3の指を離さないようにすればG#の1の指が正確につかみやすい。

弦を押えつけないよう、
Do not press down on the string.

左手の指の形を正しくし、弦を押えつけず美しい音を出す練習。

Form the correct shape of the left hand fingers, and try to produce beautiful sound without pressing down on the string.

Join the second, third and fourth fingers one after the other. Do the same with the first, second and third fingers in the following figure.

It is necessary to learn not to raise the first finger.

This can be played effectively by not raising the first finger.

Practice at the proper tempo without getting too fast.

Start the trill softly.

If the trill is begun with a big sound and strong accent, the note D will sound weak when it is played. Joachim's indication is as follows:

The chord should be played like this:

Be careful about the crescendo in the trill. This is also Joachim's indication.

restez   Keep the same position.

Point of Practice   学習の仕方

Place the first finger accurately on the D string.

The Third Movement
第三楽章

Point of Practice　　　学習の仕方

This solo part must be studied very carefully with beautiful and cheerful expression in mind. Start playing with the middle part of the bow.

このソロの部分は，美しくかつ軽快な表現を十分に研究しなければならない。弓の中央あたりから弾きはじめるのがよいと思う。

Play each of these notes lightly and try to express the contrast between the delicate legato and staccato.

この1つずつの音を美しく軽快な音で弾き，デリケートなレガートと美しいスタッカートとのコントラストを出すようにしてほしい。

Staccato in Allegro ma non troppo and staccato in Andante grazioso are so different in character that they must be made clearly contrasted in tone color.

アレグロ　マ　ノン　トロッポのときのスタッカートとアンダンテ　グラツィオーソのときのスタッカートはその性質が違うので音色などに変化をつけなければならない。

弓の下半あたりから弾きはじめる。
Start playing with the lower third of the bow.

要熟練
Adequate practice is necessary.

Practice this eighth note with short bowing, using the middle part of the bow.

この8分音符は弓巾せまく，弓の中央で練習して確実にすること。

またはスラーをつける。
or with a slur.

Point of Practice　　学習の仕方

Note: When the first finger is shifted from the third position to the fifth, pay attention to the shape of the left hand. If the angle of the little finger to the fingerboard is not like this: ⟩— but like this: —⟨, it means that the correct position is not secured yet.

A wrong shape of the left hand will prevent the fingers from moving freely. Training of the left hand for the correct shape should be considered of prime importance.

注意：1の指が第3ポジションから第5ポジションへ移ったときの左手の形に注意してください。小指が指板に対して ⟩— のような角度ではなく —⟨ の形になっていなければ正しい形ではなく、正しいポジションの位置になっていないのです。

左手の形が悪い人は、指の動きが悪く、思うように弾けません。左手の形の矯正をまず第一とすべきです。

Those who play this figure faster than the correct tempo will also play the following part too fast. Learn to play at the correct tempo.

これが正しいテンポではなく、速くなってしまう人は次のところでも速くなり、乱れて弾けなくなります。正しいテンポで弾く練習をしてください。

Point of Practice　　学習の仕方

Notice that f is indicated for the first two measures and fp leggiero for the following two measures. Training is especially necessary here. Although the indication is staccato for both pairs of measures, f should be played loudly with long bowing while p must be played with short bowing almost like spiccato. In other words, for p there is more elasticity of the bow with short bowing, and in the case of f the bowing should be more like legato. The indication fp means that f should immediately be followed by p, thus amounting to a kind of accent.

注意：表現上の注意としては、はじめの2小節がfで、その次の2小節がfp leggiero（軽く、やわらかく）という指示がしてあることです。この表現はとくに訓練が必要です。同じスタッカートでもfの場合は弓巾を大きくつかい音量を出し、pの場合は弓巾をせまく、スピッカートに近いような弾き方にする。つまり弓巾せまくかつ弓の弾力をよけいつかい、fのときはそれよりもよけいレガートに近いような弾き方です。fpはfのすぐあとpで弾くことで、これにより一種のアクセントが生まれるわけです。

Only the first D and F♯ are played f, immediately followed by p. Then the succeeding figure, which descends gradually, should be played decrescendo. Read the score as groups of four measures.

はじめのD、F♯だけをfで弾いて、次からすぐpにし、しだいに下行音型ですからデクレッシェンドして弱めていく。楽譜4小節ずつ見てください。

ゆっくり弾き正確なポジションの練習をする。
Play slowly and learn to attain an accurate position.

ここでヨアヒムは次のように弾いてもよいという指示をしている。
Joachim gave an alternative indication here. This part may be played as follows:

After accurate placement of fingers is attained, then play with *fp* at first and try to make the leggiero smooth.

正確に押えられるようになった後，最初に*fp*をつけ，leggieroで美しい表現の練習をしてください。

Note: Carefully read the note at B and pay attention to the shape of the left hand.

注意：ポジション下行の場合にBの注意事項をよく読んで左手の形に注意すること。

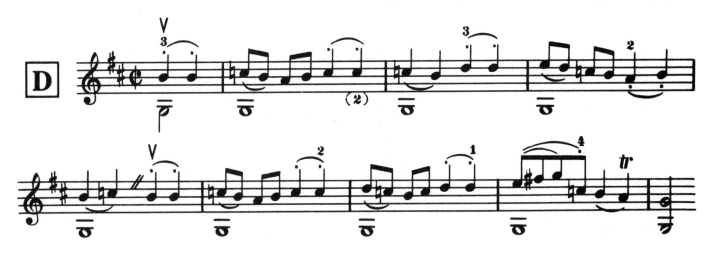

Point of Practice　学習の仕方

Practice this melody on the D string correctly.
Pay special attention to the position of the left hand and to the shape of the fingers. Don't start to play before you have learned to fix the left hand firmly after the position shift.

D弦上のこの美しいメロディーを単音で正しく弾く訓練を行ないます。
左手の位置，指の形に特に注意し，ポジションの移動で左手がしっかり定まらないうちに弾かないようにしてください。

次は一番訓練の必要なところです。
Training is especially necessary for the following part:

Point of Practice　　学習の仕方

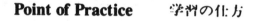

The note G pressed by the third finger is likely to be played too high in pitch. Try to get accurate pitches.

　3の指で押えるGの音が高くなりやすいから注意し，正確にする訓練。

Start playing with the upper end of the bow.

弓の先の方で弾きはじめる。

This bowing is indicated by Joachim, but here I give my own bowing for reference because I find his indication causes me some difficulty.

これはヨアヒムの弓づかいですが，私の弓には少し表現上の無理があり，次のように試みているので参考までに記しておきます。

Point of Practice　　学習の仕方

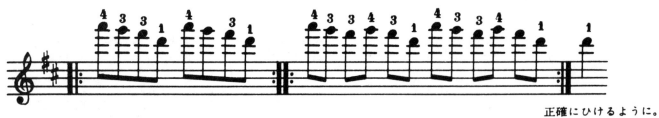

正確にひけるように。
Learn to play accurately.

自分の納得のいく美しいトリルの速さまで練習のこと。

Continue practice until you attain the speed at which you can play the trill to your satisfaction.

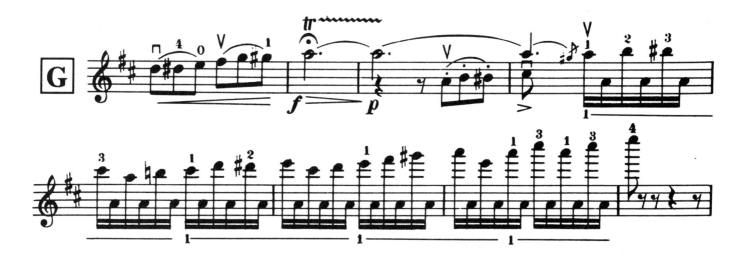

Point of Practice　　学習の仕方

Learn to place the first finger accurately without raising the second finger.

2の指を押えたままで1の指を正確に押える練習。

この形を押えるように1の指を準備する
Prepare the first finger for this note.

次にこの形を弾けるようにする訓練が必要。
Then learn to play this figure.

このポジションのときの左手の正しい形を忘れず、親指はバイオリンの胴の肩のところに位置する。

In this position, with the correct shape of the left hand in mind, place the thumb at the shoulder of the body of the violin.

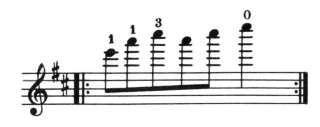

以上十分熟練したのち、Ｇを音楽的にも技術的にも立派に弾く練習をしてください。

Pupils must acquire enough skill for the above points before proceeding to practice Ｇ so that they may play well both musically and technically.

Point of Practice　　学習の仕方

Training for changing strings is necessary for this part. If excessively long bowing is used, beautiful sound cannot be expected and speed cannot be attained. A different bowing is given below for study of changing strings. This bowing may be adequate for expressing the melody effectively.

ここでは移弦の訓練が必要です。また弓巾を大きく使いすぎるとよい音が出ませんし，速度がおそくなりやすいのです。
次に移弦の練習のために他の弓づかいを参考に記しておきます。旋律をよく表現するためにこの弓づかいも良いのではないかと思います。